The Permanent Establishment of Peace

The Permanent Establishment of Peace

AL LIPOLD

THE PERMANENT ESTABLISHMENT OF PEACE

This book is written to provide information and motivation to readers. Its purpose is not to render any type of psychological, legal, or professional advice of any kind. The content is the sole opinion and expression of the author, and not necessarily that of the publisher.

Copyright © 2018 by Al Lipold

All rights reserved. No part of this book may be reproduced, transmitted, or distributed in any form by any means, including, but not limited to, recording, photocopying, or taking screenshots of parts of the book, without prior written permission from the author or the publisher. Brief quotations for noncommercial purposes, such as book reviews, permitted by Fair Use of the U.S. Copyright Law, are allowed without written permissions, as long as such quotations do not cause damage to the book's commercial value. For permissions, write to the publisher, whose address is stated below.

Printed in the United States of America.

ISBN 978-1-949746-10-5   (Paperback)
ISBN 978-1-949746-11-2   (Digital)

Lettra Press books may be ordered through booksellers or by contacting:

Lettra Press LLC
18229 E 52nd Ave.
Denver City, CO 80249
1 303 586 1431 | info@lettrapress.com
www.lettrapress.com

Contents

I.	Introduction	1
II.	War	6
III.	Hatred	10
IV.	Oppression	13
V.	Justice	17
VI.	Peace	20
VII.	Rights	23
VIII.	On Whose Side Is God?	30
IX.	Final Thoughts	38
	Index	45

I. Introduction

A critical question for the long-term survival of humankind is this: can peace be permanently established? A question that follows is, can hatred and oppression be reduced to a level consonant with such an ideal?

Pope John Paul II (May 1920-April 2005) composed the following prayer with the permanent establishment of peace in mind:

> Mary, Queen of Peace, save us all, who have so much trust in you, from wars, hatred and oppression. Make us all learn to live in peace, and educate ourselves for peace, do what is demanded by justice, and respect the rights of every person, so that peace may be firmly established.

Over the past few years, I have made note of thoughts I've come across in various media that have touched on the issue. These thoughts reflect the thinking of a wide and eclectic range of people, including such figures as Winston Churchill, Alexander Haig, Marcus Aurelius, Ann Coulter, King Abdullah II of Jordan, Mike Huckabee, and George W. Bush. I have chosen to write about what such public figures have observed.

Why write? Caroline Joy Adams touched on this point in her book *The Power to Write:*

> We write because we want to connect with others on deep levels; to cross bridges of culture, of space, and of time with our words; and to know that our words matter to others and, thus, that we matter-that we have made a difference to others.

An "excellent" purpose in life, as she pointed out.

Having thus stated the underpinnings of my thesis and my motivation in writing about it, allow me to expand on the question: can we human beings do what is demanded by justice for all people regardless of sex, color, ethnicity, religion, and place or situation on this earth? Is it possible for all to respect the rights of all?

If so, then it seems possible to me that peace can be permanently established on this earth.

As we well know, there are today, in many parts of the world, people who are living as if in centuries past. But times have changed around these people. It is now a different world from the one in which they and their forebears grew up. Science and technology have enhanced life. Education that would allow all people on earth to profit from this enhancement is not only possible but also available. Such learning should not be denied to anyone.

A model for me in believing this is Oliver Wendell Holmes, an American physician, poet, professor, and author. He said,

> Greatness is not where we stand, but in what direction we are moving. We must sail sometimes with the wind and sometimes against it, but sail we must, and not drift at anchor.

To move as this great thinker suggests, people must be free. I recall learning, as a boy, about the five freedoms featured in the First Amendment to the US Constitution: speech, press, religion, petition, and assembly. Freedom to worship God is, thus, among our greatest American blessings. This freedom, I believe, is at the heart of the possibility of peace.

In contrast to our good fortune, it has been reported that nearly a third of the world's population (2.2 billion people) lives in countries where religious persecution increased between the years 2006 and 2009. As we often read in the news, India and China are among the worst offenders in social harassment or government restrictions on religion. As we've also seen, religious violence, especially against Coptic Christians, has recently convulsed Egypt.

In pursuit of my thesis in this essay, I will try to compare various levels of religious freedom around the world. I've got something of a yardstick for these comparisons for I've read both the Bible and the Koran. As I've suggested, I also read a lot that comes to my attention in public media. In this latter regard, I want to bring to your attention an e-mail I received recently. It's purported to have this or that source, but that is a matter of contention, so I won't go into it because the point made is the issue.

In this e-mail, whoever the author is, a transcendent story is told, which may not even need an authenticated source. Let me sum it up:

A German who before World War II owned a great deal of industrial proper ty was asked after the war how many German people were true Nazis.

"Very few people were Nazis," he said, "but many enjoyed the return of German pride, and many more were too busy to care. I was one of those who just thought the Nazis were a bunch of fools. So the majority just sat back and let it happen. Then, before we knew it, they owned us and we had lost control and the end of the world had come."

This story has the ring of truth, does it not? The silent majority, confronted by fanaticism, tended to look away and hope for the best. So please take note: like fog in Carl Sandberg's poem, hate comes in on little cat feet. This seems to me to be the case with Islam today. The majority doesn't know any better than to accept the abridgment of their freedom.

We must find a way to counter this situation without violence.

In my own view, listening to the wisdom of John Paul II is the way. Relevant questions in this regard posed in *The Word among Us,* a Christian magazine, recently caught my attention:

Can we make room in our homes and in our hearts for people who speak a different language? Whose skin is a different color? Who suffer from a disability? Who come from a different culture?

In the small fraction of time that is allotted to us on this earth, will we struggle to establish peace or drift once again into war? I am thinking about the kind of war that kills millions, the kind of war that destroys cities, nations, and perhaps, civilization and mankind itself. The choice is ours, I believe. As individuals, in the manner of the Germans in World War II cited above, we might not wish to face up to that fact. But it is a fact. And I think in our hearts, we know it.

It is interesting to note what Alexander III of Macedon, commonly known as Alexander the Great, 357-323 BC, thought about time. By the age of thirty, he had created one of the largest empires of the ancient world. He was never defeated in battle. He died at a very young age.

On his death bed, Alexander summoned his generals and told them his three ultimate wishes:

1. The best doctors should carry his coffin;
2. The wealth he has accumulated (money, gold, precious stones.) should be scattered along the procession to the cemetery.
3. His hands should be let loose, hanging outside the coffin for all to see!!

One of his generals who was surprised by these unusual requests asked Alexander to explain.

Here is what Alexander the Great had to say:

1. I want the best doctors to carry my coffin to demonstrate that, in the face of death, even the best doctors in the world have no power to heal;
2. I want the road to be covered with my treasure so that everybody sees that material wealth acquired on earth, stays on earth . . .

3. I want my hands to swing in the wind, so that people understand that we come to this world empty handed after the most precious terror of all is exhausted, and that is TIME.

Winston Churchill famously said, "Never give in, never give in, never, never, never-in nothing, great or small, large or petty-never give in except to convictions of honor and good sense."

I hope in this essay to foster some of Mr. Churchill's great spirit in the cause of continuing world peace. To begin, let me bring to your attention some thoughts about war.

II. WAR

Even before history was recorded, the world knew war. It is not difficult to show the endlessness of it and the terrible cost in human lives. Quick reading-in my dictionary, in *Wikipedia,* and of stories in the news media, as well as perusal of relevant books-has provided me with data and observations that I will summarize and share to give you a reminder of our terrible past and of what is going on now and is in the works even as I write. In reading, please have in the back of your mind my question and my thesis: will there ever be an end to the carnage? It is up to you and me to involve ourselves in ending it.

Merriam-Webster Dictionary says simply that "war is a state or period of open and declared armed fighting between states or nations, a state of hostility, conflict . . . a struggle between opposing forces for a particular end."

I went to *Wikipedia* for a more extensive definition and a look at the history of human conflict. In a couple of pages that follow here, I will sum up my learning from that quarter.

In all cases of war, at least one participant in the conflict perceives the need to either psychologically or materially dominate the other. The perceived need for domination often arises from the belief that either an ideology is so incompatible or a resource so scarce as to threaten the fundamental existence of one group experiencing the need to dominate the other group.

Before the dawn of history, war likely consisted of small-scale raiding. Half the dead found in a cemetery in Nubia, along the Nile, dating to twelve thousand years ago, died of violence.

Wikipedia lists 137 wars in recorded history. To give you a sense of the loss of human life in these wars, following here are casualty figures I selected at random from the data.

- 75,000-200,000- the conquest of Alexander the Great (336-323 BC)
- 2,000,000-Second Punic War (218-204 BC)
- 3,000,000-7,000,000-Yellow Turban Rebellion, China (184-205)
- 36,000,000-An Shi Rebellion, China (755-763)
- 2,000,000-Mahmud of Ghazni's invasion of India (1000-027)
- 100,000-1,000,000-Inca civil war (1529-1532)
- 3,500,000-6,000,000-Napoleonic Wars (1804-1815)
- 618,000-970,000 (including 350,000 from disease)-US Civil War (1861-1865)
- 20,000,000-World War I (1914-1918)
- 2,500,000-3,500,000- Korean War (1950-1953)
- 23,384-Indo Pakistan War of 1971
- 1,000,000-Iran-Iraq War (1980-1988)
- 800,000-1,000,000-Rwandan civil war (1990-1994) And then we come to World War II. How terrible!

Estimates for the total casualties of World War II vary, but most suggest that some sixty million people died, including about twenty million soldiers and forty million civilians. The Soviet Union lost about twenty-seven million people, about half of all World War II casualties. (Note in comparison that about four hundred thousand American combatants died plus relatively few noncombatant citizens.) Since a high proportion of the Russians killed were young men, the postwar Soviet population was forty-five to fifty million smaller than post-1939 projections would have led one to expect. About one million citizens died during the 872-day siege of Leningrad alone.

This was the largest death toll in a single city in the war, but of course, noncombatants died in many, many cities in World War II.

The pursuit of war has become more terrible with the enhancement in means of causing death. Poison gas as a chemical weapon was principally used during World War I and resulted in an estimated 91,198 deaths and 1,205,655 injuries. Various treaties have sought to ban its further use. Nonlethal chemical weapons, such as tear gas and pepper spray, are widely used, sometimes with deadly effect. Land mines have been, and still are, a scourge. Tanks and other armored vehicles have replaced horse-drawn vehicles of war.

In 1947, in view of the rapidly increasingly destructive consequences of the newly developed atom bomb, Albert Einstein remarked, "I know not with what weapons World War III will be fought, but World War IV will be fought with sticks and stones."

Another aspect of modern warfare is the uncertainty about the ownership and sponsorship of conflict in the world. Former vice president Dick Cheney observes in his book *In My Time*,

> The first war of the twenty-first century wouldn't simply be a conflict of nation against nation, army against army. It would first and foremost be a war against terrorists who operated in the shadows, feared no deterrent, and would use any weapons they could get their hands on to destroy us.

Terrorists most often come without national responsibility.

A June 17, 2013, article in the *New York Times* underscores the array of weapons and technology coming into play in modern warfare. It notes first that in the Battle of the Coral Sea in World War II, American and Japanese carriers squared off, deploying aircraft as far-reaching fighting devices. Today, the concept of extension has led to development of cyber warfare and deployment of drones. Cyber technology allowed the Stuxnet attack on Iran's nuclear weapons program. Where the attack came from is still not clear. Drones, of course, made pinpoint attacks on terrorists.

"These advances," said the *Times* article, "will require policymakers to rethink the economic, political and moral calculus."

"I would say that the next decade is perhaps one of the most crucial in human history," said Claudia Dreifus, *New York Times* columnist, in her book *Scientific Conversations*. "There are so many things coming to a head simultaneously. The population, the environment, the energy crunch, and, of course, the dangers of a nuclear war."

We have come a long way since the cannonball. Now we have to contend with nuclear, chemical, and biological weapons that can wipe out large segments of our population in mere moments plus the development of cyberwarfare and evolution of drones.

The cost over the years, just to Americans alone, has been devastating. "Over 43 million Americans went to war of some kind in our nation's history," said Mike Huckabee in his book *A Simple Government*. "Of that amount 1.2 million gave their lives for the rest of us."

Let me conclude my observations on war by quoting General Omar Bradley, chief of staff of the US Army in World War II. He commented after the war:

> We have too many men of science, too few men of God. We have grasped the mystery of the atom and rejected the Sermon on the Mount. The world has achieved brilliance without wisdom, power without conscience. Ours is a world of nuclear giants and ethical infants. We know more about war than we know about peace, more about killing than we know about living.

Stopping the killing will involve insight, courage, and tenacity of all of us.

III. Hatred

Talking about hatred is unpleasant, but one must consider it when pondering how to attain peace in the world.

First of all, what is hatred? *Wikipedia* describes hatred as an intense feeling of dislike that may occur in a wide variety of contexts-hatred of oneself, of other people, of entire groups of people, of people in general, even of existence itself. *The Penguin Dictionary of Psychology* defines *hate* as a "deep, enduring, intense emotion expressing animosity, anger, and hostility towards a person, group or object."

In a sense that we may not choose to think about every day, we are all targets of hatred-every one of us. Targets include people of every race, gender, age, ethnicity, nationality, religion, sexual orientation, social class, political affiliation, and every other distinction that might be considered by some as a liability.

The Conservative Handbook observed,

> People that have never met you hate you with every fiber of their being. They hate you because you are free. They hate you because you represent to them everything they want but can never have because they're slaves to an oppressive and consuming philosophy of hatred that drives them to want to die taking your freedom rather than winning their own.

Terrorist organizations, the *Handbook* asserted, "show clearly the death wish that feeds them. Terrorism springs from hatred, and it generates isolation, mistrust, and closure-distancing the terrorist from rational influences. Violence is added to violence in a tragic sequence that exasperates successive generations, each one inheriting the hatred which divided those who went before.

In *john Paul IL The Great Mercy Pope,* John Paul II was quoted, "Terrorism is built on contempt for human life." And from the same book, it was said,

> Those who kill by acts of terrorism actually despair of humanity, of life, of the future. In their view everything is to be hated and destroyed. Terrorists hold that the truth in which they believe or the suffering they have undergone is so absolute that their reaction in destroying even innocent lives is justified. Terrorism is often the outcome of that fanatic fundamentalism that springs from the conviction that one's own vision of the truth must be forced upon everyone else

Most animosity is rooted in envy. *The Conservative Handbook* observed,

> There are people who hate everything we stand for. To them, America is wicked, perverted, and arrogant. They see us as the enemy of the world, the antagonist of the downtrodden, despite the fact that we give more in foreign aid than any other country on earth. They want us destroyed.

In the book *Decision Points,* one of President George W. Bush's inaugural speeches was quoted:

> After the shipwreck of communism came years of relative quiet, years of repose, years of sabbatical, and then there came a day of fire.

"We have seen our vulnerability," Bush's speech continued, "and we have seen its deepest source. For as long as whole regions of the world simmer in resentment and tyranny-prone to ideologies that feed hatred and excuse murder-violence will gather and multiply in destructive power, and cross the most defended borders, and raise mortal threat. There is only one force of history that can break the reign of hatred and resentment, expose the pretensions of tyrants, and reward the hopes of the decent and tolerant, and that is the force of human freedom.

"We are led by events and common sense to one conclusion-the best hope for peace in our world is the expansion of freedom in all the world, with the ultimate aim of ending tyranny in the world."

Jesus identified the command to love God. He then placed the second commandment, to love one another, on a par with the command to love God (Matthew 22:34-40). The command to love one another refers to all persons without exception. Is there a better way to combat or overcome hatred?

Christians, Jews, and Muslims all worship the same God. No believer should be hated by another. God is love and so should his worshipers emulate him and love one another.

Is it possible that the presence of xenophobia, the unreasonable fear or hatred of foreigners or strangers and their culture and customs, which exists in many parts of the world, be overcome? No one had a choice as to who he or she is or where he or she came into this earth. We are all equal in the eyes of God.

Again, my thesis, we need to strive for world peace, and if we each play our part, we can attain it.

IV. Oppression

There are many forms of oppression in the world and many places where it exists. "Many countries oppress their people, including North Korea, China, Cuba, Congo, North Sudan, and if I name all the bad guys we'll run out of space in this column," Cal Thomas cracked recently in *USA Today*. I have more space here in this essay, so I'll add Afghanistan, Pakistan, Iraq, Iran, Syria, Egypt, Saudi Arabia, Somalia, Libya, and others. Like Mr. Thomas, I could go on.

Just what is oppression? *Wikipedia* described it as

> the exercise of authority or power in a burdensome, cruel, or unjust manner. It can also be defined as an act or instance of oppressing, the state of being oppressed and the feeling of being heavily burdened, mentally or physically, by troubles, adverse conditions, and anxiety. It is customarily experienced as a consequence of, and expressed in the form of, a prevailing, if unconscious, assumption that the given target is in some way inferior. In sociology, the tools of oppression include a progression of denigration, dehumanization and demonization, which often generate scapegoating, which is used to justify aggression against targeted groups and individuals.

Everyone has a free will that should not be suppressed by anyone else. Our free will should allow us to live our life as we choose-to its fullest-so long as we bring no harm to others.

There are many examples of such harm. A particularly heinous harm is violence against women. All women should be able to live their lives in freedom. Yet in many parts of the Muslim world, the contempt toward women is absolute. We're not all men and women created equal? Is a Muslim male, the fruit of a Muslim mother, any better than the woman who gave him life?

In the West, we are moving toward such freedom for women. We're not there yet, as women are the weaker sex and are therefore more likely targets of abuse, but we see light, as they say, at the end of the tunnel.

With regard to freedom, I wish to touch again on the subject of religion.

The early American patriot Thomas Paine said in his pamphlet *Common Sense,*

> You who love peace, you that dare to oppose not only oppression, but the oppressor, stand forth, let your self be heard . . . let us secure freedom and property to all men, and above all things, the free exercise of religion, according to the dictates of conscience.

Modern American observers touch frequently on religion. "No matter their religion, no matter their ethnic background, people everywhere yearn to be free," *The Conservative Handbook* said.

> Oppression is oppression, whether it is coming from a communist regime or a radical Islamic theocracy. The oppressors are the minority, their stranglehold on the people is strong. People are oppressed, not only by will, but by force.

My reading of *Even unto Death: Wisdom from Modern Martyrs,* by Jeanne Kun, reminds me that in many places around the world today, it is considered a crime to be a Christian. At this very moment, many of our brothers and sisters are experiencing discrimination, persecution, and even death for their faith.

In matters of faith, each individual should be able to exercise free will and not be persecuted for it.

Can believer's m the great Religions-Christianity, Islam, Buddhism, Hinduism, Judaism-live in harmony with one another? Can people in any area of the world freely follow their conscience regarding what they believe? We all have a free will and should be allowed to exercise it. Whatever people choose to decide with regard to faith, freedom should not be denied them.

Over time, the great religions have moved away from wrath and toward love. I can sense this movement in Islam. I recently read in *USA Today* that despite the rigidity of some imams and others who impose an inflexible interpretation of Islam on believers, the tenets of Islam actually encourage Muslims to employ their own intellect in difficult decisions. That's right. Muslims are encouraged to use their own judgment, a process Muslims known as *Ijtihad,* particularly in challenges without prior precedent. The prophet Muhammad himself endorsed this exercising of the mind, said the *USA Today* article.

Hope for continuing change reflects the changing state of the scientific world. A remark made in a local newspaper about just one country in the Middle East makes the point. "Sooner or later, Saudi Arabia has to choose what century it is in," said Richard Cohen in the *Villages Daily Sun*. "It cannot strive for the high-tech world of tomorrow and at the same time have medievalists dictate and limit the boundaries of freedom."

Other Muslim nations must face this reality too. It is a different world than that of the seventh, eighth, or ninth centuries.

Where lies the heart for change? In individual people. Martin Luther said,

> Cowardice asks the question: Is it safe? Expedience asks the question: Is it politic? Vanity asks the question: Is it popular? But conscience asks the question: Is it right? And there comes a time when one must take a position that is neither safe, nor politic, nor popular, but he must take it because his conscience tells him it is right.

Winston Churchill said in World War II,

> The day may dawn when fair play, love for one's fellow man, and respect for justice and freedom, will enable tormented generations to march forth serene and triumphant from the hideous epoch in which we have to dwell. Meanwhile, never flinch, never weary, never despair.

As so often is the case in remembered remarks by Mr. Churchill, here is a plea for courage as we face a challenge that appears to be insurmountable but perhaps-just perhaps-is a possibility: peace in the world.

V. Justice

Consideration of justice must be a factor in the search for world peace.

Justice is a moral concept of rightness based upon ethics, rationality, law, natural law, religion, and fairness and/or equity. Justice is also said to bring about the administration of what is just, as by assigning merited awards.

Justice in and of itself requires that an injured person (party or entity) be somehow compensated for a wrong done to him, her, or a legal entity. A legal entity could be a corporation, partnership, an association (political, religious, or civic), etc.

As to legal matters, we quickly think of torts; personal injuries; violations or breaches of contract; matters involving the title or ownership of property, real property, and personal property; and domestic matters, such as divorce and separation. These few matters are just the tip of the iceberg in consideration of where someone or some entity could be wronged and should be compensated.

Generally speaking, laws, statutes, rules, and regulations are enacted by a legislative body for the benefit and protection of all people. In criminal law, an accused is presumed to be innocent until either admitting guilt or being found guilty by a court of competent jurisdiction or by a jury of his peers. If found guilty, and depending on the nature and severity of the crime, the accused is punished accordingly. Justice is thereby served.

Justice should not be denied to any person because of race, color, nationality, sex, religion, lack of citizenship, etc. The denial of justice is prevalent in many nations. For example, China, North Korea, Saudi Arabia, Iran-these are some of the worst offenders.

Women, particularly, in many parts of the world, are treated as property rather than as human beings. Yet is not every person, male or female, created in the image and likeness of God? If so, women should be respected and treated as equal to men. Women should not be denied justice because of their sex. Justice cries out for equality of the sexes. Even Saint Paul, the apostle, speaking of man and wife, said, "Submit *to one another* out of reverence for Christ" (Ephesians 5:22-23). Thus, to me, Paul sees a *mutual* obligation of ethical behavior between the sexes.

Another text I considered is the Koran, where it is said,

> Justice has been the cause of all God's prophets, and God has placed the lover of justice in the hearts of his servants. Those who are upright, those who stand up for justice, form an axis of goodness about which communities of faith can and must come together. (5:25)

I found this quotation in *The Axis of Good: Muslims Building Alliances with Other Communities of Faith,* by Ingrid Mattson.

Marcus Aurelius considered the issue of justice about 1,800 years ago:

> Should obstacles arise, advance discreetly to the limit of your resources, always following where justice seems to point the way. To achieve justice is the summit of success.

He also said,

> We can never achieve justice while we set our hearts on things of a lesser value, and are content to remain headstrong and inconstant.

I found these two admonitions in *Meditations,* on page 143.

The belief that God has made us equal has always been the strongest basis on which to argue for universal justice. I read this observation in the March 21, 2011, edition of *USA Today,* and of course, this idea has resonated throughout American history.

Another commentator on justice has been former president George W. Bush. "In the struggle of the centuries," he says in his book *Decision Points,* "America learned that freedom is not the possession of one race. We know with equal certainty that freedom is not the possession of one nation. This belief in the natural rights of man, this conviction that justice should reach wherever the sun passes, leads America into the world. With the power and resources given to us, the United States seeks to bring peace where there is conflict, hope where there is suffering, and liberty where there is tyranny."

Ronald Reagan was, of course, another commentator on justice. He is quoted, in his pithy way, on page 143 of *The Notes,* his collection of stories and wisdom: "Man's capacity for justice makes democracy possible but man's inclination to injustice makes democracy necessary."

We often hear the phrase "He got away with murder." In other words, justice was not served. If an individual, group, or nation kills, torments, or imprisons people without just cause, justice is not served. If persons are killed or otherwise maltreated because of their religion or their personal beliefs, is not justice denied?

VI. PEACE

In the past seven thousand years, which is the approximate time of known recorded history, there have been seemingly endless wars among nations, tribes, religions, and other coalitions. These wars have always been followed by peace agreements that held only for a while. That is to say, the *continuation* of peace has been elusive.

Consideration of continuing peace has ancient roots.

The Roman historian Tacitus, writing a text called *Life of Agricola* about two thousand years ago, talks of a wartime leader who by choosing not to slaughter the enemy tried to establish peace:

> And when he had sufficiently terrified the enemy, by sparing them he showed them the attractions of peace.

The ancient Greek historian Herodotus tells us in his *Histories* of a royal advisor explaining to the Persian king the usual method of warfare between rival Greek city-states. The method consisted, the advisor said, of a pitched battle between massed ranks of heavily armed men. The advisor then commented on what seemed to him the sheer absurdity of Greek fighting Greek.

> Yet since they speak the same language and share the use of heralds and messengers, they should settle their differences in any way but fighting.

Some 2,500 years later, in our own time, we find similar frustration over conflict. We also find similar hope and glimmers, however fragile, of lasting peace. For example, observers once feared that tensions across the Berlin Wall as well as frictions in Northern

Ireland might never be eased. Yet in both cases, peace, however complicated, has emerged. These observations in support of hope are made in *Our Last Best Chance,* a book about the pursuit of peace by King Abdullah II of Jordan.

My point is that then and now in history, here and there on this earth, people have hoped for peace and sometimes had some effect. We are all people of the world; we share a common humanity. All people of every race, color, religion, and gender should in some way or another be involved in the quest for survival, that is to say, for the permanent establishment of peace.

> Ruth, the main character in the book of Ruth in the Old Testament, is quoted as saying, "Your people shall be my people, and your God my God." In this way, she symbolizes the reaching out that we must do. Christians, Jews, and Muslims all believe in the same God. All worship and adore him. In him they all trust. They all seek his support and guidance and pray to him for peace. Why have not the faithful of these three great religions made serious efforts to unite as friends of God in the search for a lasting peace?

There have been and are, I am sure, brilliant scholars and theologians in all these three religions who are equal to the task. But where are the leaders? Are the rifts so great, the divisions so wide, the fear of loss of power so pervasive that serious attempts at unity or even mutual thought of unity are not possible?

The tensions between Israel and Palestine have gone on much too long. *King Abdullah II* of Jordan writes in his book, *Our Last Best Chance:*

> We need to resolve immediately the final status issues: Jerusalem, refugees, borders, and security. At this point, it is our only hope of rescuing the two-state solution. There is no other option. We have no choice but to live together. Both sides have a moral responsibility to strive for peace... The alternative is more conflict and violence. The window is closing, and if we do not act soon, future generations will condemn our failure to seize this last chance for peace.

I believe it is in his *Memoirs* that former US president Richard Nixon says of the search for peace in the Middle East,

> It takes courage, a different kind of courage, to wage peace. Continuous war in the area is not a solution to Israel's survival and, above all, it is not right.

As I read in *Meditations,* almost 2,000 years ago, the Roman emperor Marcus Aurelius said,

> Think of the totality of all being, and what a mite of it is ours; and the brief fleeting instant of it that is allotted to us; think of destiny, and how puny a part of it we are. What do we do with the time allotted to us?

In reading a book by Mike Huckabee, *A Simple Government,* I was struck by this thought of his:

> Christian believers... have the confidence that, no matter how challenging things can be, the ultimate outcome will be positive and victorious. That is one reason, among many, that there should be no gloom and doom in the mind, heart, or spirit of a true believer.

Saint Paul's message in *1 Corinthians* resonates. The love that he spoke of will help lead us to continuing peace.

Our world is here, in this place, at this time. And as Yakov Smirnoff, comedian and philosopher, observed,

> You couldn't give the past to someone because it is already gone. You can't give the future because it isn't here yet. The only time you can give and experience happiness is right now. That's why we call it the present.

It is time for the political, economic, religious, military, and social leaders of the world to unite for a common purpose, that is, the permanent establishment of peace.

VII. Rights

The second paragraph of the Declaration of Independence begins with one the most well-known sentences in the English language, expressing a thought that ranks among the greatest expressions of belief expressed in the course of history:

> We hold these truths to be self-evident, that all men are created equal, that they are endowed by their Creator with certain unalienable Rights, that among these are Life, Liberty and the pursuit of Happiness.

As I have read in *Wikipedia,* this passage has come to represent a moral standard toward which the whole world should strive. It is self-evident that this will not be easy.

This difficulty is underscored by thoughts I gleaned from a book called The Bible in the Light of Christian Science, volume 1, *Genesis:*

> Today we live in a world that faces critical problems. On the *individual* scale [emphasis mine], millions of people are without shelter, have no work, live in upset family relations, are afflicted by sickness and fear and so feel plagued by hopelessness and aimlessness. *Collectively* [again, emphasis mine] our problems are [also] acute; we face the perpetual threat of nuclear war, dwindling natural resources, pollution, economic instability and political oppression.

We must look for solutions to these problems. Permanent peace would be a linchpin in the search. The focus of the search for such peace would be on securing these rights:

- The right to life, which is the first and foremost of rights The right to pursue a healthy and safe existence
- The right to become educated
- The right to freedom of speech, to voice one's opinion without the threat of arrest
- The right to participate in governmental affairs, such as voting The right to choose one's religion without government interference

Taken together, these are rights to fullest freedom. As Thomas Jefferson points out in his immortal words in the Declaration of Independence, quoted above, "The right to freedom is God-given, and not a government privilege." Is there one person or group of persons that has the right to deprive others of these rights?

Thanks to scientific advancements (e.g., computers, the Internet, cell phones, and high-speed travel), nations and individuals are closer to each other than ever before. Yet at the same time, we all have a natural tendency to consider a person of another race different, of another religion different, of another ethnic origin different. These perceptions tend to abridge rights all over the world.

Three examples (among many I could point to) are easy to find.

1. *Russia.* "Over the past decade," said an article I read in *Time* magazine, "opponents of [Russian Premier] Vladimir Putin's regime have been harassed, imprisoned, tortured and killed. But still, these men and women took to the streets, marching in the Russian winter, asking for the same things protesters around the globe have been asking for-dignity, inclusion, participation and freedom."
2. *China.* In the wake of the Arab Spring, which must have scared the heck out of the Chinese ruling class, *Time* said, "Hu & Co. have been clamping down on free speech and human rights throughout the country . . . The government has tightened Internet controls and jailed dozens of public intellectuals and human rights activists."

    In China, according to *Amnesty International,* "thousands of political prisoners are sentenced by unfair trials or no trials at all." Providing further insight into treatment of Chinese citizens, *The Conservative Handbook* says, "Endemic torture, including severe beatings, the use of electric batons and suspending victims by their arms; re-education through labor camps, imprisonment of unauthorized religious groups; forced abortion and sterilization . . . these are just [some] of the human rights violations we know about."

3. *India.* As stated in a report by *the Sisters of Notre Dame,* many women in India are mistreated. The nuns' sad observation in one particular circumstance was this:

Women accepted their home situation with passivity, not knowing the way out. They could not voice their pains and struggles since they were not united and organized. Many women were unaware of the need for education, the facilities available for health care, their need to get involved in political and social decision-making, and their own personal worth.

The situation of women in the world with respect to human rights is particularly worthy of consideration.

"If you look at what is happening to women in many parts of the world, it is tragic and terrible," Hillary Rodham Clinton observed when she was secretary of state. "Under Islamic law, husbands have the authority to beat their wives for disobedience. " The book *Muslim Mafia* asserts that "more than 80 percent of women in Pakistan suffer from domestic violence."

"Islam, in practice, clearly gives preference to men, while women are more like pieces of property," said Steven Masood in *Into the Light.*

"Even in Paradise, according to the Qur'an, there are no JOYS to be expected for women believers."

Anglican archbishop Desmond Tutu, committed to abolishing child marriage around the world by the year 2030, said in remark to the United Nations that in addition to ending child marriage, girls should become freed from poverty, ignorance, and oppression at the hands of their husbands.

> Women are helping to lead the way to their own freedom: Three women from Africa and the Middle East who symbolized nonviolent struggles to improve their nations and advance the role of women's rights were awarded the Nobel Peace Prize in 2011. Sharing the award were Liberian president Ellen Johnson Sirleaf, Africa's first democratically elected female president; her countrywoman Leymah Gbowee, a peace activist who challenged warlords; and Tawakkul Karman, a Yemeni human-rights leader seeking to overthrow an autocratic government as part of the Arab Spring movement. As reported in the *Orlando Sentinel,* the UN citation said in part, "We cannot achieve democracy and lasting peace in the world unless women obtain the same opportunities as men to influence developments at all levels of society."

In the book *Decision Points,* Laura Bush is quoted as saying, "Afghan women know, through hard experience . . . the fight against terrorism is also a fight for the rights and dignity of women."

Somewhere in my reading, I saw this:

> Every Muslim man is the fruit of a Muslim woman's womb. Is he better than the woman who gave him his life? There is no reason for supposed superiority of one sex over the other.

The issue of course transcends issues of women that I mentioned above. In my reading *The Word among Us,* I saw this:

> Every human being is a child of God, created in his own image and likeness. And this means that every person deserves to be treated with the deepest respect.

I read something by Oliver Thomas in *USA Today* that provides me with an overview of problems that impede progress in human rights. "Consider the issues that most threaten humanity's common future," he said, mentioning "global terrorism, climate change, overpopulation, and the political and social unrest caused by economic disparity." "These problems," he observed, "transcend national boundaries and beg for international solutions."

Problems continue as a modern-day plague. Yet, in my humble opinion, political leaders worldwide have generally been unwilling or unable to find solutions with regard to human rights.

But again, I do see light flickering, however faintly, at the end of the tunnel.

In President Nixon's first inaugural address, m 1969, addressing inequality in America, he said,

> No man can be fully free while his neighbor is not. To go forward at all is to go forward together. This means black and white together, as one nation, not two. What remains is to give life to what is in the law: to insure that all are born equal in dignity before man.

In an Easter message quoted in the *Villages Daily Sun,* Pope Benedict XVI prayed that all citizens, especially young people, would work to promote the common good and to build a society where poverty is defeated and every political choice is inspired by the respect for the human person.

In his book *The Notes,* Ronald Reagan stressed a point that I believe in wholeheartedly. Freedom provides *opportunity,* but each of us must participate as hard as we can in the process.

> Freedom rests, and always will, on individual responsibility, individual integrity, effort, individual courage, and individual religious faith.

We know this to be true, yet we can't seem to get traction on it. It seems as though we do the same things over and over and expect different results. Albert Einstein defined insanity as doing the same thing over and over and expecting a different result. There is an old saying, "Here I stand, poor fool that I am, as wise as I was as when I first began."

We must have faith, and we must hope that the more posltlve political sentiments of our time will evolve and prevail. But we ourselves also have to join the struggle.

Spiritual teacher Marianne Williamson has some thoughts on this subject.

> Our thoughts about the future go far toward creating it; our minds and hearts are like filaments that connect today to tomorrow, they are conduits for either the status quo or the emergence of different, hopefully more loving, possibilities. How we think and how we behave determine where we are going.
>
> We should all support the efforts of struggling people, particularly in the Third World . . . this to improve their lives through education, health care, women's empowerment, social work and spirituality.

In the Catholic magazine The Word among Us, I have read,

> How praiseworthy it is to love and to honor one another. Our friends, our neighbors and co-workers. Those who are weak and different from us. Because we are all created in the image and likeness of God. Every single soul on earth is deserving of our respect and consideration.

It has been said that the life and dignity of every person must be respected and protected at every stage and in every condition. The right to life is the first and most fundamental principle of human rights.

Muhammad is reported to have once said,

> Mankind are the family of God, and the most beloved of them to God are those who are the most excellent to His family. Not one of you believes until he loves for this brother what he loves for himself.

To lighten your burden in all this, dear reader, I will leave this chapter with a smile for you. Yakov Smirnoff, the thoughtful comic I mentioned above, has observed, "It has been said that every human being has dignity and value, no matter what their citizenship papers say."

VIII. ON WHOSE SIDE IS GOD?

The right of freedom should apply to all believers -Christian, Jew, Muslim, Hindu, and Buddhist, as well as adherents of any other religion, whether it seeks a path to my god or any other person's god. My only caveat is that no sect can have such a right if it advocates violence in support of its beliefs.

At a White House dinner, someone asked President Lincoln, "Don't you believe that the Lord is always on the side of the right?"

"I am not concerned about that," Lincoln said, "for we know that the Lord is always on the side of the right. My concern is that I and this nation should be on the Lord's side."

At the heart of this thought, I believe, is that Lincoln believed that it is people themselves who decide whether to behave as God ordains. The strictures of holy books are only guidelines.

And we do have a lot of people! Earth's population grows exponentially.

Ten thousand years ago, the population of the planet Earth was approximately one million. At about the year *5000* BCE, the world's population was about five million people. At the time of Christ, the population of the world was two hundred million. The population of the earth reached a billion around the year 1804, just after the US Revolutionary War. Today the population of the world is over seven billion.

The growing number of people in the world fascinates me. In 1927, a year before I was born, the population was only two billion.

Maybe eight billion people will be on the planet in the year 2028-the centennial of my birth.

As the population has so dramatically increased, what have we learned about the commandment "Thou shalt not kill"? Not much. Why are people and nations so dysfunctional? Although we can do nothing to change the past, we can change the future. So now is the time to act for peace.

The following quotations, excerpts, etc., touch in various ways on the subject of peace. Can we learn from such observations? Here is some glue that might help: it has been said that we should seek unity within our diversity, the blessings of wisdom in our deliberations, and the mind of God in our decisions.

Thomas Edison, the great American inventor, said that if we did all the things we are capable of doing, we would, literally, astonish ourselves.

Political leaders must have the courage to make peace for the sake of all of us. King Abdullah, in his book *The Last Best Chance,* said, "We must pray that we can overcome the hatreds and suspicions that have kept us so long divided."

Saint Augustine is quoted in *City of God,*

> Love of God and our neighbor, on these two commandments, as it is written, hang all the law and prophecies.

During Solomon's time, as I had read in the book *Jesus or Muhammad,* the Queen of Sheeba (960 BCE) said, "Peace and friendship are better and wiser; war only brings humiliation, enslaves people and destroys good things."

Some of the most exciting challenges are not met on the battlefield or legislative halls, the arena, etc., but inside the heart and the mind of an individual human being. Henry Wadsworth Longfellow said, "Perseverance is a great element of success. If you only knock long enough and loud enough at the gate, you are sure to wake up somebody."

A sobering statement was made by Bernice King, chief executive of the King Center in Atlanta, recalling a statement made by her father:

> The choice is no longer between violence and nonviolence, but nonviolence and nonexistence.

Winston Churchill said in 1941, "We learn that we are spirits, not animals, and that something is going on in space and time, and beyond space and time, which, whether we like it or not, spells duty."

Mike Huckabee had observed, "Our responsibility to others requires us to do more than just show that we tried, and that we came close. We must get results."

> All these wise sayings attempt to pierce the wall of resistance lo peace in the world. But as I observe, it is not an easy task. There are rogue nations, like North Korea and Iran, that openly indicate that war is not something of the past. They not only want to defeat their enemies, but they also want to annihilate them completely or wipe them off the face of the earth.

So there are nations that fail to follow the commandment of God.

Then-and I wish to dwell on lost souls for a moment-there are the jihadists, extremists, and terrorists, who would kill anyone to gain their objective of world dominion. I wish to put them and their behavior in perspective.

In his book *An Inconvenient Book: Real Solutions to the World's Biggest Problems,* Glenn Beck wrote:

> I have read the Koran and can tell you that I unequivocally believe that Islam is a religion of peace. The overwhelming majority [I believe at least 90 percent] of all Muslims are good, peace-loving people. [Mr. Beck then says] It is clear to me that the radicals' plan to use force and intimidation

is working. They [the extremists] have shown that they are more than willing to kill anyone, including other Muslims, who don't share their beliefs, and that has left many moderate Muslims living in fear. Muslims are not the enemy. Extremists who want to destroy democracy and create Islamist states all over the world are the enemy.

King Abdullah II of Jordan, writing in his book *Our Last Best Chance,* said,

> To comprehensively defeat terrorists, we will have to neutralize the appeal of their extremist ideology and combat the ignorance and hopelessness on which they thrive. This is not just a military battle, it is an intellectual one. And it is a battle we started a while ago.

In the book *John Paul II, The Great Mercy Pope,* John Paul was quoted as saying, "Injustices in the world can never be used to excuse acts of terrorism." He urged world religions to "work together to eliminate the social and cultural causes of terrorism" and to "take the lead in publicly condemning terrorism and denying terrorists any form of religious or moral legitimacy." He added, "The help that religions can give to peace and against terrorism consists precisely in their teaching forgiveness."

John Paul then said,

> Consequently no religious leader can condone terrorism and much less preach it. It is a profanation of religion to declare oneself a terrorist in the name of God, to do violence to others in His name. Terrorist violence is a contradiction of faith in God, creator of man, who cares for man and loves him.

In particular, John Paul said,

> I am convinced that Jewish, Christian and Islamic religious leaders must now take the lead in publicly condemning terrorism and denying terrorists any form of religious or moral legitimacy.

A few years ago, I read an article by Joe Angione in the *Villages Daily Sun* in which he observed,

> There are many reasons why the Islamic world doesn't get along with U.S. policy and American culture. Radical Muslims hate us because we represent success, wealth, freedom and opportunity that are not available in their repressive brand of Islam . . . where women are men's property, and all must follow in great fear for their lives, a twisted theocracy that would impose a monstrously cruel "serfdom" on the entire world.

As stated by Thomas Friedman in the *New York Times,* too many young Muslims are dealing with a powerful inner conflict. They are raised to believe that Islamic religion and culture are superior, yet they come to see that the Muslim world is behind the West, mired in poverty and political impotence.

Question: how can a Muslim retain his identity as a Muslim yet be open to modernity? It has been said that Islam refers not only to the act of submission but to its consequence, that is, peace *(salam).*

Then there are terrorist governments. One Muslim who speaks to this issue and even questions Islam itself is Ayaan Hirsi Ali, a Somali-Dutch-American writer. She is a Muslim who has lived in Somalia, Kenya, and Saudi Arabia. In her book *Infidel,* she said that in Saudi Arabia,

> people had their heads cut off in public squares. Adults spoke of it. It was a normal routine thing that after the Friday noon prayer you could go home for lunch or you could go and watch the executions. Hands were cut off Men were flogged. Women were stoned. In the late 1970s Saudi Arabia was booming, but though the price of oil was tugging the economy into the modern world, its society seemed fixed in the Middle Ages.

She added,

> Most Muslims never delve into theology, and we rarely read the O!iran; we are taught it in Arabic, which most Muslims can't speak. As a result people think Islam is about peace. It is from these people, honest and kind, that the fallacy has risen that Islam is peaceful and tolerant. But I could no longer avoid seeing the totalitarianism, the pure moral framework that is Islam. It regulates every detail of life and subjugates free will. This Islam, as a rigid belief system and a moral framework, leads to cruelty.

There is hope, she said, in believing that Islamic culture, like Christian culture, will evolve. She said:

The West underwent a period of religious warfare and persecution, but society freed itself from the grip of violent organized religion. I Assumed-I still assume-that the same process could occur among the millions of Muslims. We Muslims could shed our attachment to those dogmas that clearly lead to ignorance and oppression.

Because of recent uprisings (civil wars) in Libya, Egypt, and Syria, it is obvious that all Muslims are not on the same page. Deep down and individually, many have a strong desire for freedom- freedom of their own destiny and freedom of choices in life.

Gareed Zakaria observed in *Time* magazine,

> The danger in the Middle East is not that Islam corrupts, but that power corrupts. A more open and democratic system is no panacea, but it will begin to create a more normal, modern politics for the region . . . and that will move the East forward and not back

In *Nomad,* I read, "If the Muslim mind can be opened to the idea that the Koran was written by a committee of men over the 200 years that followed Muhammad's death, the 'read-only' lock on the Holy Book can be opened ."

A similar point might be made about the Bible and the evolution of the people who have read it over time and how it is interpreted more pacifically today than in prior centuries.

In my opinion, the ayatollahs, imams, and clerics who support violence are stuck in a rut. They must come to realize that we are not living in the seventh century. Times have changed. It is now the twenty-first century.

The Koran states, "God changes not what is in a people, until they change what is in themselves." As I read this, I was struck by its similarity to Abraham Lincoln's point: God offers the principles; we people take it from there. And, hopefully, we evolve.

Christianity had its holy wars, but then it had its reformation. In my opinion, Islam must have its own reformation.

In the book *Hot, Flat, and Crowded,* Thomas Friedman, a foreign-affairs columnist for the *New York Times,* said,

> No one knows how the Iraq saga is going to end. But there are two things I know for sure: One is that the need to drive reform in the Arab Muslim world is as vital as ever: Educational reform, empowerment of women, religious modernization and more consensual politics. The other that no matter what happens in Iraq, we, the United States, are not going to invade another Arab Muslim country in the name of reform any time soon. We need to find another way to partner with people there.

As I reflected in this essay, bigotry-the stubborn and complete intolerance of any creed, belief, or opinion that differs from one's own-must end. And any person should be able to be a Muslim, Jew, Christian, Buddhist, Hindu, or whatever (within ethical reason) because he or she individually chooses to be so and not because a particular religion is forced upon him or her. Any person should be free to change to another religion if so inclined.

Terrorists could do with a little soul-searching. Are they truly Muslims, or are they using Islam to further their political goals? And are the supporters of terror backing Islam or rogue elements? If the terrorists were true Muslims, I believe they would not be terrorists. The problem is, people drawn to terrorism are notably young and brainwashed to believe in killing people.

Can the murder and suicide they perpetrate be stopped? Islamic law does not condone these behaviors.

In *Decision Points,* George W. Bush said suicide is said to be forbidden in Islamic ethics. There is a direct and explicit text in the Koran and hadith on the issue of suicide. Two very well-known Koranic verses speak on the issue: "Do not cast yourself into destruction" and "Kill not yourself "

According to Islamic creed, as I have read in the book *Living with Grief,* God is the creator of human life; therefore, a person does not own his or her life and hence cannot terminate it. I had also read in this book, "Suicide is a major sin in Islam. God is the only one who has the right to end the life of a person."

Nor is the kind of senseless killing embodied in suicide bombing sanctioned in Islamic tradition. As I read in *Our Last Best Chance,*

> Almost all Muslims are aware of the tradition set in the early days of Islam in the seventh century by the first Muslim Caliph, Abu Baker Al Sediq, whose instructions to his armies were to *not* kill [emphasis mine] women or children or elderly people.

Time and literacy will have a lot to do with Islamic behaviors. We can involve ourselves in encouraging literacy to shorten the time

IX. Final Thoughts

In her book *World on Fire,* Amy Chua said,

> Market Capitalism is the most efficient economic system the world has ever known. Democracy is the finest political system the world has ever known and the one most respectful of individual liberty. Working hand in hand, markets and democracy will gradually transform the world in a community of prosperous, war-shunning nations . . . . In the process, ethnic hatred, religious zealotry and other backward aspects of underdevelopment will *be* swept away.

Further, she said,

> To level the playing field in developing societies . . . will be painfully slow process . . . In the short term, investment in education, and other forms of human capital can contribute.

In America and in the West, we do not claim social, moral, political, and economic perfection. And neither can they who are from the East, Middle East, and other parts of the world. However, we must remember that we are all entitled to freedom regardless of our race, religion, political association, sex, etc.

Our world is big, and there is room within it for all people to prosper. All should be given the opportunity to make the attempt.

All should be allowed to focus their attention to achieve the desired results.

The Permanent Establishment of Peace

The following comments by well-known people relate to the subject of peace.

It has been said that knowledge, understanding, and respect, if they prevail, will make a positive difference in the world, "peace by peace."

Nelson Mandela said that education is the most powerful weapon you can use to change the world.

Jimi Hendrix said that when the power of love overcomes the love of power, the world will know peace.

President Eisenhower said at the end of his second term, regarding our children and their spiritual heritage, "We want democracy to survive for all generations to come."

George Washington said,

> It is the duty of all nations to acknowledge the providence of Almighty God, to obey His will, to be grateful for His benefits, and humbly to implore his protection and favor.

In a book about evolution called *Life's Solution*, I read this:

> Life has no option but to carry on. It must always play the best hand it can no matter how poor and disastrous the hand might be, and no matter who or what offers the challenge.

An item of Useless Knowledge, as printed in the *Villages Daily Sun*, observed, In the last 3,500 years, there have been only 230 years of peace throughout the civilized world.

Sun Tzu said, 2,500 years ago,

> Winning 100 battles is not the acme of skill. To subdue the enemy without fighting is the acme of skill.

"On August 14, 1941, President Franklin Delano Roosevelt and Prime Minister Winston Churchill signed The Atlantic Charter. In it they said they were convinced by two global wars in the span of twenty years that they had an obligation to try to check mankind's destructive impulses. Such impulses, they thought, could destroy mankind itself. They hoped to see established a peace which would afford an assurance that all people, in all lands, might live out their lives in freedom from fear and want. More than seventy-two years later their hopes have not been achieved." I read this observation in *American Legion Magazine*.

In a sonnet by J. G. Holland titled "Wanted," he said,

> God give us men. A time like this demands strong minds, great hearts, true faith and ready hands; men whom the lust of office does not kill; men whom the spoils of office cannot buy; men who possess opinions and a will; men who have honor; men who will not lie . . . tall men . . . who live above the fog in public duty and in private thinking.

We also need strong women-women like Malala Yousafzai and Aung San Suu Kyi. Both of these women were featured in a *Time* magazine list of "100 Most Influential People of the World." We need such women because many young girls are tested, and they need role models. At the age of fifteen, Malala was shot in Pakistan by a Taliban gunman. The Taliban later said she was shot to teach a "lesson" to anyone who had the courage to stand up for education, freedom, and self-determination, particularly girls and women. I understand that Chelsea Clinton, daughter of the former president and of the former secretary of state, is writing a memoir to raise awareness about the sixty-one million children around the world who are not in school.

As to Aung San Suu Kyi, the following is from an article about her by Madeline Albright, former secretary of state:

> In 1990 the Burmese military refused to recognize the electoral victory of Aung San Suu Kyi's pro-democracy party. Five years later, Suu Kyi was released from house

arrest. She was firm in her demands: real democracy, freedom for political prisoners, an end to government by fear. In 2011, the authorities began to back down. Censorship was reduced; prisoners were released. Suu Kyi was elected to parliament. Aung San Suu Kyi's bravery in defying and defeating repression gives hopes to all who cherish liberty.

I noted a few observations in Thomas L. Friedman's *Hot, Flat, and Crowded:* We should be "united and propelled by a common purpose, not a common enemy." Also, "the hour is late. The stakes couldn't be higher, the project couldn't be harder, the payoff couldn't be greater." Also, "imagine if we could tap into the creativity and innovative capacity of the world's poorest people. Imagine if we could empower them with the tools and energy they need to really compete, connect and collaborate. It would lead to an explosion-from science and technology to art and literature." To "what could be more patriotic, capitalistic, than that?"

Pope Benedict XVI had said, "God of Peace, bring your peace to our violent world . . . comfort us and console us, strengthen us in hope, and give us the wisdom and courage to work tirelessly for a world where true peace and love reign among nations and in the hearts of all."

He encouraged Arab Spring nations, especially Egypt, to build just and respectful societies. He prayed that China's new leadership may "esteem the contribution of the religions, in respect for each other, to help build a fraternal society of that noble people."

He urged the North African region to build societies "founded on justice and respect for the dignity of every person." He prayed for the return of peace in Mali and harmony in Nigeria, where he recalled "savage acts of terrorism continue to reap victims, particularly among Christians." These quotes came to me in my reading of the *Villages Daily Sun.*

The following two quotes are taken from *Nostra Aetate,* proclaimed by Pope Paul VI on October 28, 1965:

> The Church, therefore, exhorts her sons, that, through dialogue and collaboration with the followers of other religions, carried out with prudence and love and in witness to the Christian faith and life they recognize, preserve and promote the good things, spiritual and moral, as well as the socio-cultural values found among these men ... This sacred synod urges all to forget the past and to work for mutual understanding and to preserve as well as promote together for the benefit of all mankind, social justice and moral welfare, as well as peace and freedom.

Pope Francis I recently urged economic, political, and religious leaders (Christian, Jewish, Muslim, Buddhist, Hindu, Sikh, and Jain) not to allow omens of destruction and death to accompany the advance of this world.

> Today, amid so much darkness, we need to see the light of hope and to be men and women who bring hope to others.

> To protect creation, to protect every man and every woman, to look upon them with tenderness and love, to open up a horizon of hope, is to let a shaft of light break through the heavy clouds.

In conclusion, thank you for reading! I end by quoting some of Pope John Paul II's remarks taken from the book *john Paul II: The Great Mercy Pope*.

> There is a "duty to defend the dignity of every human person" (p. 55).

> In fact, love of God and love of one's neighbor are inseparable. (p. 88)

> Apart from the mercy of God there is no source of hope for mankind. From Divine Mercy, which brings peace to hearts, genuine peace flows into this world, peace between different people, cultures and religions. (p. 187)

May Mary obtain this gift of Divine Mercy for all of humanity so that the individuals and peoples who are particularly tormented by hostility and fratricidal war may overcome hatred and build concrete attitudes of reconciliation and peace. (p. 221)

My question is this: can we move toward permanent peace? God guides us, but acting on his principles, we must seek permanent peace on our own. We must decide, and we must act. There is no other way.

INDEX

A

Abdullah II (king) 1, 21, 33
Africa 26
Albright, Madeline 40
Amnesty International 24
Arab Spring 24, 26, 41
armies 37
Aung San Suu Kyi 40, 41
Axis if Good, The 18

B

battlefield 31
Battle of the Coral Sea 8
beliefs 19, 30, 33
believers 15, 22, 25, 30
biological 9
Buddhism 15

C

change 26
chemical 7, 8, 9
children 37, 39, 40
China 2, 7, 13, 18, 24, 41
Christianity 15, 36
Christians 3, 12, 21, 41
commandments 31
conflict 6, 8, 19, 20, 21, 34
conscience 9, 14, 15
Conservative Handbook 10, 11, 14, 25
contempt 11, 13
Coptic Christians 3
courage 9, 16, 22, 27, 31, 40, 41
crime 14, 17

D

death 4, 7, 10, 14, 35, 42
Declaration of Independence 23, 24
dehumanization 13
democracy 19, 26, 33, 38, 39, 40, 41
dignity 24, 26, 27, 28, 29, 41, 42
discrimination 14
domestic 17, 25

E

education 25, 28, 38, 39, 40
Egypt 3, 13, 35, 41
Ellen Johnson 26
empowerment 28, 36
extremists 32, 33

F

faith 14, 15, 18, 27, 28, 33, 40, 42
freedom 2, 3, 10, 12, 13, 14, 15, 16, 19, 24, 26, 30, 34, 35, 38, 40, 41, 42
free will 13, 14, 15, 35
Friedman, Thomas 34, 36

G

Gbowee, Leymah 26
God 2, 9, 12, 18, 19, 21, 24, 26, 28, 30, 31, 32, 33, 36, 37, 39, 40, 41, 42, 43

– 45 –

H

hate 3, 10, 11, 34
health care 25, 28
Herodotus 20
Hinduism 15
Histories 20
history 6, 7, 8, 9, 11, 19, 20, 21, 23

I

ignorance 26, 33, 35
Inconvenient Book, An 32
India 2, 7, 25
injuries, personal 17, 19, 25
injustice 19
Islam 3, 15, 25, 32, 34, 35, 36, 37
Islamic law 25, 37
Israel 21, 22

J

Jesus or Muhammad 31
Jews 12, 21
John Paul II (pope) 1, 3, 11, 33, 42
Jordan 1, 21, 33
Justice v, 17, 18

K

Koran 3, 18, 32, 36, 37

L

law 17, 25, 27, 31, 37
liberty 19, 38, 41
life 2, 7, 11, 13, 14, 24, 26, 27, 28, 35, 37, 42
Life of Agricola 20
Life's Solution 39
Lincoln, Abraham 36
literacy 37
love 12, 14, 15, 16, 22, 28, 39, 41, 42

M

mankind 4, 40, 42
Meditations 18, 22
moral framework 35
Muhammad 15, 28, 31, 35
Muslim Mafia 25
Muslims 12, 15, 18, 21, 32, 33, 34, 35, 37

N

nationality 10, 17
Nazis 3
neighbor 27, 31, 42
New York Times 8, 34, 36
Nobel Peace Prize 26
nonviolence 32
nuclear weapons program 8

O

Our Last Best Chance 21, 33, 37
overpopulation 27

P

peace 1, 2, 4, 5, 9, 10, 12, 14, 16, 17, 19, 20, 21, 22, 23, 26, 31, 32, 33, 34, 35, 39, 40, 41, 42, 43
persecution, religious 2
poverty 26, 27, 34
power 4, 9, 11, 13, 19, 21, 35, 39
property 14, 17, 18, 25, 34

R

race 10, 17, 19, 21, 24, 38
reformation 36
religion 2, 3, 10, 14, 17, 19, 21, 24, 30, 32, 33, 34, 35, 36, 38
religious 2, 3, 17, 22, 25, 27, 33, 35, 36, 38, 42
resources 18, 19, 23
rights 1, 2, 19, 23, 24, 25, 26, 27, 28

Ruth 19
Ruth (biblical character) 21

S

Saudi Arabia 13, 15, 18, 34
self-determination 40
sexes 18
Sir leaf, Ellen Johnson 26
social work 28
societies 38, 41
soul-searching 37
suicide 37

T

Tacitus (historian) 20
tensions 20, 21
terrorism 11, 26, 33, 37, 41
terrorist organizations 10
terrorists 8, 32, 33, 37
truth 3, 11
tyranny 11, 12, 19

U

United Nations 25
United States of America 19, 36
US Revolutionary War 30

V

Villages Daily Sun 15, 27, 34, 39, 41
violence 3, 6, 10, 11, 13, 21, 25, 30, 32, 33, 36

W

war 3, 4, 5, 6, 7, 8, 9, 22, 23, 31, 32, 38, 43
warfare modern 8
West 14, 34, 35, 38
Wikipedia 6, 7, 10, 13, 23
World War I 7
World War II 3, 4, 7, 8, 9, 16

Y

Yousafzai, Malala 40

Edwards Brothers
Malloy Thorofare, NJ
USA December 4, 2013

Can peace in our time be permanently established? Can the hatred and oppression that abounds on this earth become a thing of the past? Can the people on this earth be taught to live in peace? Can they do what is demanded h>y justice and respect the rights of every person?

It has been said that we know, that we can change things. The world's leaders, religious, political, military, economic, scholars etc., could and should focus their attention on the ultimate goal of achieving world peace. It can be done. It should be done. It must be done.

AL LIPOLD, Attorney at Law

Born on November 1 1928 son of an immigrant miner.

Served as a World War II veteran, August 1946 to March 1948 in the US Revolutionary War United States Marine Corps.

Attended John Carroll University and Cleveland State University

(Cleveland Marshall Law School) and awarded JD Degree.

Admitted to the Bar in 1955 in the State of Ohio, Employed as a trial attorney for 28 years in the Cuyahoga Country, Ohio, prosecutor's office.

Served as First Assistant Prosecutor for five years.

I'm a member of a several veteran's and fraternal organizations. I am the father of three sons and six grandchildren.

www.ingramcontent.com/pod-product-compliance
Lightning Source LLC
Chambersburg PA
CBHW050204130526
44591CB00034B/2142